the story of the U.S.A.
by Franklin Escher, Jr.

Book 3
America Becomes a Giant

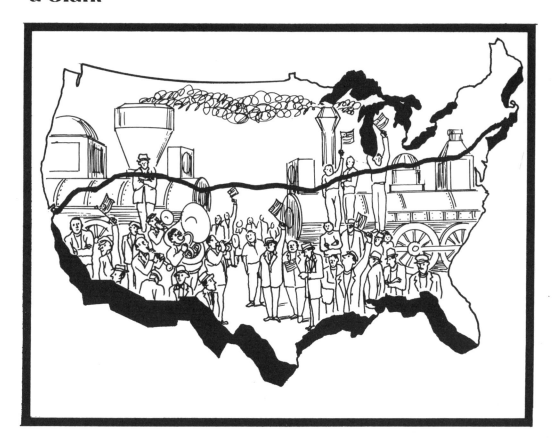

Educators Publishing Service
Cambridge and Toronto

Educators Publishing Service
800.225.5750
www.epsbooks.com

Printed in U.S.A.
ISBN 0-8388-1635-5

5 6 7 8 9 PAH 08 07 06 05 04

Table of Contents

For the Student

Welcome to the world of American history. You are going to read about our country's past. History is filled with exciting stories and interesting people. This book will tell you about some of them. It can also help you practice ways to read and study that you can use in all your classes, not just in history class.

Before you start working in this book, you will need to know how it is put together. Each chapter is arranged into parts that take you along one step at a time. If you follow the directions, you will be able to read and learn the material without any trouble.

To begin with, there are pictures and sometimes maps at the start of each chapter. By studying them, you will get an idea of what you are going to be reading about.

Next, there are a few vocabulary words. This vocabulary section gives meanings and pronunciations for some words that will appear in the chapter. The letters in CAPITALS are parts of the word which are accented, or said the loudest:

example = eg-ZAM-pul

Turn next to the chapter story. At the beginning are two or three questions, just beneath the title. These give you some hints about the main ideas and help you start thinking *before* you read. Keep these questions in mind, and look for the answers as you read.

Some words in the chapter story are printed in heavy black type called **boldface**. These are the words from the vocabulary page. Some other words and names are printed in *italics*. That is a signal to look at the right-hand column of the page if you need help in pronouncing them.

One more thing to look for is a black dot ●. Most chapters are divided into sections, with a dot to show that a main section has come to an end. That should be your signal to stop and think back over the paragraphs in that section. Try to tell yourself the main ideas that were built up. Ask yourself WHAT happened, WHO did it, and WHY. A quick review like this helps you take the facts and ideas from a book and put them into your own words. That is the best way of all to study.

At the end of each chapter you will find exercises to do. Don't think of these as a test. They are designed to help you review the most important facts and ideas in the chapter. As you work along through the book, think carefully about what you are reading. This will help you to do the exercises without having to look back at the chapter.

Exercise A always deals with the main ideas. Ideas are even more important than facts. If you know the main ideas of a story, you understand its meaning. For example, it is just as important to know *why* France sold Louisiana to the United States as it is to know *when* it was done.

Exercise C, D, or E is a vocabulary review. This exercise should be easy. It is designed to help you strengthen and build your vocabulary by giving you extra practice with the words from the first page of the chapter. You will see some of those words again and again in later parts of the book. The last exercise in each chapter is called "Think About and Discuss in Class." Here, you and your classmates can begin to relate the past to the present and to your own lives. You can look for the lessons that history can teach us. Why do wars start? Why do people starve? How can the world be made a happier place to live in?

History teaches us lessons, and it is fun to read. You'll enjoy the stories of the first explorers and settlers of America. Some of them were heroes, some villains, and some were a little of both. Pick out your favorites and talk about them in class.

As you turn these pages, you will find yourself reading faster and faster. Keep it up! Within a short time, you will be moving easily through this book. It will help make you a better reader and a better student.

President Abraham Lincoln was murdered by John Wilkes Booth. Booth had sympathized with the South in the Civil War.

Getting Ready for Chapter One

Here are three vocabulary words that are used in the story of what happened after the Civil War. Study these definitions so you will know what each word means when you see it in your reading.

villain   (VIL-en)   A person who does evil things.

impeach   (im-PEACH)   To have a trial and accuse a high official of bad conduct in office. If the president of the United States is impeached, he is tried by the Senate, with the chief justice of the Supreme Court acting as judge.

reconstruction (ree-kon-STRUK-shun)   Rebuilding and restoring; the period, 1865-1877, in United States history when the North rebuilt the South.

Andrew Johnson of Tennessee followed Lincoln as president. Johnson did not go to school as a boy. When he grew up, his wife Eliza helped him learn to read and write.

Some Southern whites were so angry at the rights granted to Blacks that they formed the Ku Klux Klan. Klansmen beat and killed Blacks and carpetbaggers.

After the War

Who killed Abraham Lincoln?
Why did people hate President Johnson?
Who were the "carpetbaggers"?

It was a time to celebrate. All across the land, Americans gave thanks that the Civil War was over. In the North, there were parades, parties, and fireworks. It was April 1865.

President Abraham Lincoln and his wife, Mary, went to see a play at Ford's Theater in Washington. The president was laughing and enjoying himself. Suddenly, a man came up behind where Lincoln was sitting. He pulled out a pistol and shot the president in the head. Then with a wild cry, the murderer escaped from the theater.

President Lincoln died the next morning. His killer was an actor named John Wilkes Booth, who had sympathized with the South in the Civil War. Soldiers later found Booth hiding in a barn. They killed him when he refused to give himself up.

The victory celebrations in the North stopped. America's great and kind leader was gone. In the defeated South, there was sorrow, too. Lincoln had promised to welcome the Southern people back to the United States. The South had lost a sympathetic friend. •

Vice-president Andrew Johnson of Tennessee became our next president. Johnson was not a popular leader. The North disliked him because he came from the South. The South disliked him because he had sided with the North in the war. He did not think the South should leave the Union.

President Johnson tried to carry out Lincoln's plan to return the South to the Union, but he quickly ran into trouble with Congress. Many Republicans in Congress hated the South. They were afraid that if the South were back in the Union, with representatives in Congress, Republican power would be threatened. Here is what Congress did, against Johnson's wishes:

1. It took away the vote from Southern leaders who had fought in the Civil War.

2. It said they could not hold public office. The South lost many of its best leaders because of this rule.

3. It wrote the Fourteenth Amendment to the Constitution. This amendment made Blacks American citizens. Every Southern state had to approve the amendment before it could return to the Union.

4. It passed the Fifteenth Amendment, which gave Blacks the right to vote and hold public office.

5. It sent soldiers to the South to carry out its orders. •

Giving Blacks in the South the rights of citizens was the fair thing to do, but the Republicans in Congress had another reason. With the Black vote on their side, they thought they could control Congress and the whole country.

Because of these rules, some of the new state governments in the South were poorly run. Neither the Blacks nor the whites who served in them had much education or *experience*.

eks-PEER-ee-ents

Some shrewd Northerners also saw a way to get rich in the South. They hurried there carrying cheap suitcases made of carpet cloth. People called them "carpetbaggers." These **villains** made friends with the freed slaves. They bought votes and got themselves elected to public office. While the South was trying to get itself *organized*, the carpetbaggers made as much money as they could from *business* and government.

OR-guh-nyzed
BIZ-nuss

The Southern whites who had lost their vote were furious. Some of them formed a secret club called the Ku Klux Klan. Klansmen dressed in long white robes with pointed hoods to scare people. They rode on horseback at night, beating and killing carpetbaggers and Blacks. •

President Johnson *continued* to fight Congress with his veto power. Congress became so angry that it **impeached** the president. Johnson was tried in court for "high crimes." The president was not guilty of any crimes. All he had done was to disagree with Congress. Johnson finally won his case and stayed in office. He is remembered as the only American President to be impeached.

kun-TIN-yood

The Civil War had left the South in *ruins*. Large cities were destroyed by gunfire. There was not enough food to eat. Both Blacks and whites often had to beg for enough food to stay alive.

ROO-inz

In 1865, Congress set up the Freedmen's *Bureau*. The Bureau gave food and clothing to needy Southerners. It also started schools and colleges for freed slaves.

BYOOR-ow

Reconstruction came to an end in 1877. By that time, the North was tired of trying to manage the South. "Let the South run its own affairs," people said. Federal troops were taken out of the South by President Rutherford B. Hayes.

Left to itself, the South turned against the Blacks. Although the Blacks could not be made slaves again, they were "put in their place." If Blacks tried to vote, they were threatened and beaten. State laws were passed that took away their civil rights. Life for the Blacks became almost as bad as it had been under slavery.

Answer these to review the main ideas.

A.

1. How did President Lincoln die? _____

_____

2. Why was the South especially sorry about Lincoln's death? _____

_____

3. What did Americans think of President Johnson? _____

_____

4. Why did Johnson have trouble with Congress? _____

_____

5. Why did carpetbaggers rush to the South? _____

_____

6. What was the Ku Klux Klan? _____

_____

7. Why was President Johnson impeached? _____

_____

8. What happened to the freed slaves after the North left the South?

_____

_____

B.

Circle True or False.

T F 1. An actor named John Wilkes Booth murdered President Lincoln.

T F 2. The South was glad that President Lincoln was dead.

T F 3. President Johnson's plan to bring the South back into the Union was different from Lincoln's.

T F 4. Carpetbaggers were honest Northerners who were anxious to help the South recover.

T F 5. After Reconstruction, the freed slaves lost many of the rights they had gained.

C.

Circle the right answer to finish each sentence.

1. The Civil War ended in

   a. 1860   b. 1863   c. 1865

2. Before the Southern states could return to the Union, they had to

   a. ratify the Fourteenth Amendment
   b. pay 5 million dollars
   c. punish their leaders

3. The Fourteenth Amendment gave Blacks

   a. American citizenship
   b. land grants
   c. education benefits

4. President Johnson was impeached for

   a. "high crimes"
   b. murder
   c. lying

5. Congress tried to help the South by starting

   a. the Red Cross
   b. the Freedmen's Bureau
   c. the Ku Klux Klan

Choose one of these words to fit each sentence below.

D.

   impeach   villain   reconstruction

1. After the Civil War, the North tried to rebuild the South through a

   program of _____.

2. People considered John Wilkes Booth a _____

   because he killed Lincoln.

3. Congress said President Johnson was guilty of "high crimes" and

   _____ ed him.

Think about and discuss in class.

E.

How successful was Reconstruction? What did the country gain from

it? How much did it help Blacks?_____

_____

_____

Why was it important that President Johnson won his case and stayed

in office? _____

_____

_____

While Andrew Johnson was president, the United States bought Alaska for $7,200,000. The President's many enemies thought it was a big mistake. They called Alaska "Johnson's polar garden." Alaska has an important natural resource. Do you know what it is? Do you know of any others? _____

_____

_____

_____

_____

The inventions of Thomas Edison changed people's lives. Edison invented the electric light and the phonograph.

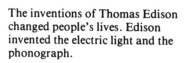

AMERICAN RAILROADS IN 1890

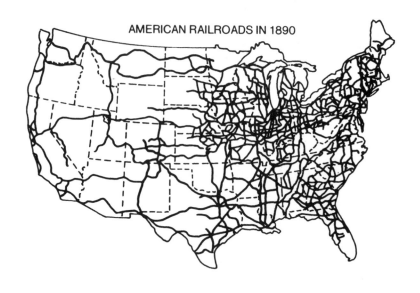

After the Civil War many railroads were built. People in different parts of the country had much more contact with each other.

New factories were built to manufacture new products. There were new jobs for men, women, and children.

The first railroad to cross the continent from the Atlantic to the Pacific Ocean was built in 1869. Now people could travel between New York and California in less than a week.

Getting Ready for Chapter Two

2

Here are six vocabulary words that are used in the story of America's growth after the Civil War. Study these definitions so you will know what each word means when you see it in your reading.

trans-continental	(trans-kon-tih-NEN-tul)	Stretching all the way across a continent.
towering	(TOU-er-ing)	Very, very high.
manufacture	(man-yoo-FAK-chur)	To make a product by machine in a factory.
monopoly	(muh-NOP-uh-lee)	Being the only person or company that has complete control over what happens to a product — how much it costs, how it is made, etc. Running a whole industry oneself.
billion	(BIL-yun)	One thousand million.
profit	(PRAH-fit)	Money made after all expenses have been counted.

America Keeps Growing

How did the railroads help bring Americans together again?

What were some of the inventions made after the Civil War?

How did John D. Rockefeller become rich?

Picture two trains coming slowly toward each other on the same railroad track. One train comes from the East, the other from the West. Crowds cheer and bands play when the two engines touch, nose to nose. The first coast-to-coast railroad has been built across the United States.

That happened in 1869, near Ogden, Utah. The **transcontinental** railroad was built by two companies. The Central Pacific Company started building east from Sacramento, California. Most of its workers were Chinese. They had the *courage* to lay track across the **towering** Sierra Nevadas. The Union Pacific Company started building west from Omaha, Nebraska. Most of its workers were Irish immigrants. The transcontinental railroad joined the East and the West by rail in the heart of America. Passengers could travel between New York and California in less than a week, a trip that used to take months. •

KUR-ij

The Civil War had torn the United States apart. When the fighting ended, Americans tried to get the country back together again. More railroads were built. Some of them joined the North and the South. One ran from New England to Georgia and Florida. Another went from Louisiana up to Illinois. Northerners and Southerners traveled together and did business with each other. These contacts helped bring the North and the South together once more.

Wherever the railroads went, towns grew up. Stores and hotels were built to serve travelers. Factories were built near railroads so that products could be more easily sent to other cities. In this way, our country grew and developed. •

Americans used their minds and hands to invent many useful products. It took workers to **manufacture** these products, and salespeople to sell them. New businesses meant more jobs and money for most people. New inventions made life easier and more fun.

One of our country's greatest inventors was Thomas Edison. He was born in Ohio in 1847. When he was a child, his teachers thought he was a slow learner. He stayed in school only three months. Then his mother took him out and taught him herself. His mind was always full of ideas.

Edison invented the electric voting machine in 1868, when he was only twenty-one years old. He invented the phonograph in 1877. His greatest invention was the electric light bulb, in 1879. *Imagine* how this changed people's lives! He also made the first movies, in 1893.

Alexander Graham Bell was another important inventor. Bell wanted to invent a machine that would send human voices over wires by electricity. In 1876 his experiments worked. Bell invented the telephone. •

People in business did very well after the Civil War. Many became millionaires. John D. Rockefeller made a *fortune* in oil. He did it by buying up other companies until he controlled the whole oil industry. Then Rockefeller charged whatever he wanted for oil. He had a **monopoly** on the oil industry.

FOR-choon

Andrew *Carnegie* did the same thing with steel. He became the ruler of the steel industry. When he sold his company in 1901, he was worth 1.5 **billion** dollars. This was more than the whole wealth of the United States one hundred years earlier.

KAR-neh-gee

Big businesses produced large amounts of goods and services. Americans who could afford to buy and use them lived well. But business also did some harm. In their fight to make greater **profits** companies spent less money making their products. One way they lowered costs was to pay low wages to workers and make them work longer hours.

In time, workers learned how to protect themselves. Then owners and workers got along better together. We shall see how this happened in the next chapter.

Answer these to review the main ideas.

A.

1. Who built the first transcontinental railroad? _____

_____

When? _____ How was the railroad built? _____

_____

2. How did the railroads bring Northerners and Southerners together

again? _____

_____

3. How did the railroads help the country grow? _____

_____

_____

4. What were some of Thomas Edison's inventions? _____

_____

5. How did business help the United States? _____

_____

How did it hurt it? _____

_____

Circle the right answer to finish each sentence.   B.

1. The companies that built the transcontinental railroad met each other near

   a. San Francisco,   b. Ogden, Utah   c. Omaha,
      California   Nebraska

2. The workers for the Union Pacific Railroad were mostly

   a. Swedish   b. Japanese   c. Irish

3. The workers for the Central Pacific Railroad were mostly

   a. Chinese   b. Native Americans   c. Italians

4. As a boy, Thomas Edison was

   a. very bright in   b. average   c. a slow learner
      school

5. Alexander Graham Bell invented

   a. the telephone   b. the cotton gin   c. graham crackers

6. After the transcontinental railroad was built, passengers could travel from California to New York in

   a. a year   b. a week   c. six months

Draw a line from the person in the first column to what he did in the second column.   C.

Andrew Carnegie   Invented the electric light bulb

Thomas Edison   Invented the telephone

Alexander Graham Bell   Had a monopoly on the oil business

John D. Rockefeller   Made a fortune out of steel

Choose one of these words to fit each sentence below.

| manufacture | monopoly | transcontinental |
| billion | profit | towering |

1. A railroad stretching all the way across a continent is a _____ _____ railroad.

2. The giant stood _____ over the small child.

3. One thousand millions, or 1,000,000,000, is one _____.

4. If you own all the candy stores in town, you have a _____ _____ on the candy business.

5. After she paid all her workers the factory owner had a _____ of $45,000 left to enjoy.

6. New machinery made it easy to _____ engines.

Think about and discuss in class.

Have you ever ridden on a train? _____ Are railroads an important way of traveling now? _____ Are they more or less important than they used to be? _____ Why? _____

_____

Suppose you had a monopoly on all skateboard manufacturing in your town. Would you charge higher prices than are charged now? Would it be fair to the public if you did? What might happen if you kept raising your prices? _____

_____

_____

_____

_____

New farm machinery planted and harvested crops faster than people working by hand could.

Samuel Gompers headed the American Federation of Labor. He thought representatives from business and labor should try to reach agreements by compromise.

Workers went on strike to try to force factory owners to improve conditions. They wanted more pay and shorter hours.

Getting Ready for Chapter Three

3

Here are five vocabulary words that are used in the story about business and labor unions. Study these definitions so you will know what each word means when you see it in your reading.

massacre   (MAH-suh-kur)   The cruel killing of a number of usually helpless people.

dignified   (DIG-nih-fyd)   Having a proud, serious manner and behavior.

harvest   (HAR-vest)   To gather up.

society   (suh-SY-eh-tee)   A group of people formed into an organization that has a goal. Also a community, a nation.

candidate   (KAN-dih-dayt)   Someone who is running for office.

Big Business and the Labor Unions

What does going on strike mean?

Why did the farmers get angry with the railroads?

From sunrise until dark, six days a week, in the late 1800s many Americans worked in factories. When the week was over, they were paid four or five dollars. This was supposed to be *enough* for them to live on for another week.

ee-NUF

Of course, prices were lower a hundred years ago. A pretty good meal in a *restaurant* cost thirty-five cents. But a weekly salary of just a few dollars was still not enough. To make enough money to live on, whole families went to work — men, women, and children. If a worker asked his boss for a raise, he would often be turned away. "If you don't like working here, go somewhere else," the boss might say. There were far more workers than jobs. Anyone who had a job was thought to be lucky.

RES-tur-ahnt

One worker alone could not force an owner to improve conditions in a factory. The power of one worker alone was not enough. However, many workers who got together could use their power to work or not to work. If a boss would not listen to them or make changes they asked for, they could go on strike — stop working. If workers went on strike, the factory would have to close. No goods could be manufactured and the owner's sales would drop. This loss of money would force the owner to give in. This seemed to be the best way for workers to get what they wanted. •

In 1869, workers formed a big labor union. It was called the Knights of Labor. At first, it was like a secret club. The members did not want their bosses to know that they belonged to a union. They were afraid their employers would fire them if they found out.

The Knights of Labor demanded a working day of just eight hours. They also asked for more pay. In 1885, when the Wabash railroad refused their demands, they went on strike and won. More and more workers joined the Knights, until there were 700,000 members.

In 1886, some workers in Chicago were on strike, demanding that the work day be no longer than eight hours. On May 3, police fired on strikers, killing one and wounding several others. The next evening, workers held a meeting in Haymarket Square to protest. One hundred eighty police were sent to the square. Suddenly, someone threw a bomb at the police. Seven policemen were killed and at least sixty more were wounded. The bomb thrower was never found, but several workers were charged with crimes. Some were hanged. The American people were not sympathetic. They blamed the violence on all labor unions, including the Knights. After the Haymarket **massacre**, the Knights of Labor began to die out. •

In that same year, 1886, a new union, the American Federation of Labor, was born. Its leader was Samuel Gompers, a **dignified** Englishman. Gompers' union was a federation of crafts unions. Its goals were to improve workers' wages and working conditions, and to get shorter work days.

Gompers was opposed to violence. His plan was to have representatives from business and labor talk their problems over. Then they would reach an agreement or compromise. This method of settling differences is called collective bargaining. It is still used today. •

Life was changing for workers on farms, too. Machines were being used more and more. Farm machinery pulled by horses rolled over the earth on wheels. The machines planted and **harvested** crops much faster than people working by hand could. As a result, many farm workers lost their jobs.

For a while farmers were pleased with the new railroads. They depended on them to take their crops to market. But then the railroads raised their rates higher and higher. Many farmers could not afford to pay the rates. Hard times came to the farms.

In 1867 a government clerk named Oliver H. Kelley started a **society** for farmers called the Grange. Kelley traveled around the country *urging* farmers to join. Thousands of farmers became members of the Grange.

UR-jing

Then Kelley put this power to work, just as the Knights of Labor had done. He told his members to *pressure* the federal and state governments to help the farmers. The Grange voted for **candidates** who promised to regulate the railroads. Many farmers were elected to office. In time, laws were passed that helped the farmers. Several states forced the railroads to lower their *freight* rates for farmers.

PREH-shur

FRAYT

Over the years, business and labor have opposed each other many times. They have learned to get along better than they once did.

Answer these to review the main ideas.

A.

1. How well were workers paid one hundred years ago? Did they earn enough to live on? _____

_____

2. Why did the workers organize labor unions? _____

_____

3. What did the unions do to win benefits from business?

_____

_____

4. What was the Haymarket Massacre? _____

_____

5. What is collective bargaining? _____

_____

_____

6. Why did the farmers challenge the railroads? What steps did they

take? How well did they succeed? _____

_____

Circle True or False.

T F 1. The workers of a hundred years ago made a great deal of money.

T F 2. The workers discovered that if they worked together, they had power to bargain with the factory owners.

T F 3. Samuel Gompers believed in collective bargaining.

T F 4. The farmers depended on the railroads to take their crops to market.

T F 5. Oliver H. Kelley told the farmers to leave the federal and state governments alone.

Circle the right answer to finish each sentence.

1. The Knights of Labor was started in

    a. 1865   b. 1869   c. 1876

2. The Haymarket Massacre took place in

    a. Chicago   b. Cleveland   c. Cincinnati

3. The American Federation of Labor was headed by

    a. Oliver H. Kelley   b. Rutherford B.   c. Samuel
                             Hayes   Gompers

4. When business and labor try to reach a settlement, they sometimes take part in

    a. striking   b. collective   c. voting
                        bargaining

5. The Grange is an organization of

    a. business people   b. farmers   c. factory workers

Choose one of these words to fit each sentence below.

D.

candidate   dignified   massacre

harvest   society

1. Perhaps some day you would like to be a _____ for President of the United States.

2. People who work together for a purpose are sometimes called a _____.

3. If soldiers kill a lot of people in a town, we say there has been a _____.

4. Most kings and queens look very _____.

5. Farmers are happy when they _____ a big crop.

Think about and discuss in class.

E.

Perhaps someone in your family, or a friend, belongs to a labor union.

Ask him or her what it's like to belong to a union. _____

_____

_____

Should the government make rules about wages and prices in American industry and agriculture? Or should business and labor decide?

_____

_____

_____

Once most Americans lived on farms. Today, most Americans live in cities and towns. What has happened to our farms? Why do we have fewer and fewer farmers? _____

_____

_____

_____

Farmers and sheep raisers moved onto the Plains. They built houses out of sod because they had no trees for wood.

Native Americans on the Plains fought hard to try to keep their land. General Custer tried to force them back on the reservation in the Battle of Little Bighorn. Custer and his army were wiped out.

More and more soldiers were sent to the Plains. Native Americans could not fight them all and were massacred. Those who were left were forced onto reservations.

Cowboys from Texas brought herds of longhorn cattle to the Plains. The trip was called the Long Drive.

Getting Ready for Chapter Four

4

Here are six vocabulary words that are used in the story about problems on the plains. Study these definitions so you will know what each word means when you see it in your reading.

plains	(PLAYNS) Level stretches of land without trees. Prairies.
stampede	(stam-PEED) A sudden wild rush by frightened animals who are out of control.
crazed	(KRAYZD) Wild; mad; not normal.
cavalry	(KAV-ul-ree) Soldiers on horseback or in armored cars or tanks.
dashing	(DASH-ing) Lively and full of energy; having lots of spirit. Having clothes or manners that are smart.
ambush	(AM-bush) A surprise attack by people who have been lying in wait.

Problems on the Plains

Where are the Great **Plains**?
What was the Long Drive?
Who were Tatanka Yotanka and General Custer?

After the Civil War, one large part of America was still Native American land. This part was called the Great Plains. It stretched west through the Dakotas into the Rocky Mountains. It reached from Mexico all the way north to Canada.

In the 1840s Americans in covered wagons traveled across the Plains to the Pacific coast. After the California gold rush, the discovery of gold and silver in Colorado and Nevada attracted white settlers. The transcontinental railroad brought still more settlers to the Plains.

Texas cowboys came to the Plains in the 1860s. They drove big herds of longhorn cattle north to *Abilene*, Kansas, and other railroad towns on the Plains. The cowboys sold their cattle, which were then shipped by railroad to Chicago and other large cities.•

A-buh-leen

The trip north from Texas was called the Long Drive. Cowboys rode beside thousands of cattle formed into long lines, like a parade. The animals' hooves pounded the ground like thunder, and they kicked up clouds of dust. Sometimes the cattle became frightened and tried to escape or **stampede**. Then it was up to the cowboys to drive them back into line. It was a very *dangerous* job. **Crazed**, stampeding cattle trampled many cowboys and their horses to death.

DAYN-jur-us

During the 1870s millions of cattle were driven north. The cowboys found that the cattle grazed well on the Great Plains. They turned some animals loose, and those animals spread out across the Plains.

Big ranches were started for the Plains cattle to live on. The ranch owners branded the cattle with their own special mark. The brand on each animal showed who owned it. Later, the owners fenced in their cattle with barbed wire.•

Farmers and sheep raisers also moved onto the Plains. Since there were no trees for wood, they built their homes with sod. Sod is ground covered with grass. The pioneers cut the sod into bricks and piled them on top of each other. The floors of the homes were plain dirt.

As more and more people moved onto the Plains, the Native Americans living there became angry and bitter. Buffalo, which they needed for food as well as for housing, bowstrings, *lariats*, and fuel, were being destroyed. Diseases of the white men were spreading. Once again the white men broke their promises and took away Native American lands. When the Native Americans protested, soldiers were sent to force them to move to reservations. Reservations were lands set aside for them by the government.

LA-ree-uts

Two leaders who would not give in were Tatanka Yotanka and Tashunca Uitco of the *Sioux* people. (They are sometimes called Sitting Bull and Crazy Horse.) In 1876 they led about 2500 Native Americans off the reservation to the Little Bighorn River, in Montana. There they fought a last battle for the right to stay on their own land and live the way they had lived for generations.

General George Custer and his excellent U.S. **cavalry** were sent to force the Native Americans back on the reservation. Custer was a Civil War hero. He was a **dashing** horseman who wore his long, red-gold hair over his shoulders. Always anxious for a fight, he disobeyed orders and attacked Tatanka Yotanka.

The Native Americans were ready and waiting. Custer saw only a small force, but most of the men were hidden behind rocks and hills. When Custer charged, he was immediately surrounded and under attack. Custer and his whole army of 267 soldiers were killed in the **ambush**. This victory is called the Battle of Little Bighorn.

Newspapers all over the United States reported the battle. They called it Custer's Last Stand because the soldiers fought until all were killed.

More soldiers were sent to the Great Plains. More Native Americans were driven off their land and massacred. The Battle of Wounded Knee, in 1890, marked the end of the fighting.

Most of the Native Americans were moved onto reservations. Their lands grew smaller and smaller. Those who lived on the Plains were hunters, and were not suited for life on a reservation. There were fewer and fewer of them. The Native American way of life was dying out.

Answer these to review the main ideas.

1. Where were the Great Plains? _____

_____

2. Where did the Long Drive start? Where did it end? _____

_____

3. How did the ranch owners tell which animals belonged to them?

_____

_____

4. What kind of homes were built on the Great Plains? _____

_____

SOO

A.

5. Why did the Native Americans of the Great Plains become angry?

_____

_____

6. What happened at the Battle of the Little Bighorn?_____

_____

_____

7. How did the fighting on the Great Plains come to an end? _____

_____

Circle the right answer to finish each sentence.

1. Texas cowboys came to the Great Plains in the

   a. 1840s   b. 1850s   c. 1860s

2. The trip made by cowboys and cattle from Texas north to the Great Plains was called

   a. the Trail of Tears   b. the Long Drive   c. the Oregon Trail

3. Native Americans were massacred at the Battle of

   a. the Little Big-horn   b. Abilene, Kansas   c. Wounded Knee

4. The Battle of the Little Bighorn was fought in

   a. 1863   b. 1876   c. 1890

5. A reservation is a place where

   a. Native Americans live   b. cattle are shipped to market   c. Texas cowboys ride

Circle True or False.

T   F   1. The Great Plains were settled by Americans before the Civil War.

T   F   2. Gold and silver were found in Colorado and Nevada after the California gold rush.

T   F   3. The cowboys drove their cattle all the way from Texas to Chicago.

T   F   4. Texas cattle grazed well on the Great Plains.

T   F   5. Tatanka Yotanka commanded the Native Americans at the Battle of Little Bighorn.

D.

Choose one of these words to fit each sentence below.

stampede   crazed   ambush

plains   cavalry   dashing

1. Flat, grassy pieces of land without trees are called

   _____.

2. Soldiers who fight on horseback or from tanks are called

   _____.

3. Tatanka Yotanka's hidden men caught Custer and his cavalry in

   an_____.

4. A person who is lively or who dresses and acts smartly

   is _____ .

5. The animals' eyes were _____ with rage.

6. It's a good idea to get out of the way when animals begin to

   _____.

E.

Think about and discuss in class.

Do you watch "cowboy and Indian" programs on TV or in the movies?

Is either side treated unfairly? If so, how? _____

_____

_____

How did the railroads help the cattle business on the Great Plains?

_____

_____

_____

_____

What kind of a man was George Custer? The story gives you several hints or clues. How good a soldier was Custer? Can a soldier be a hero without being a good soldier?_____

_____

_____

Was Tatanka Yotanka a good leader? Find out what happened to him in his later life. _____

_____

_____

_____

_____

_____

_____

During the 1800s millions of immigrants from Europe came to America. They were looking for freedom and for good jobs.

Getting Ready for Chapter Five

5

Here are five vocabulary words that are used in the story of a nation of immigrants. Study these definitions so you will know what each word means when you see it in your reading.

opportunity   (op-ur-TOO-nih-tee)   A good chance to do something.

natural   (NACH-ur-ul REE-sor-sez) Useful things supplied by
resources   nature, such as land, water, and minerals.

natives   (NAY-tivs)   People born and raised in one place or country.

Scandinavian   (skan-dih-NAY-vee-un)   Having to do with the countries of Iceland, Denmark, Norway, Sweden, and Finland.

slums   (SLUMZ) Poor, broken-down, crowded, and unhealthful housing in a city.

Chinese and Japanese immigrants usually settled on the West Coast. Many Chinese worked on the building of the transcontinental railroad.

Children of immigrants went to school, where they learned the language and customs of America.

A Nation of Immigrants

Why would people want to leave a country they grew up in and come to a new land?

Which immigrants were brought here against their will?

Were your parents born in the United States? What about your grandparents? Unless you are a Native American, if you go back far enough, you will find that your ancestors came here from another country. They were immigrants.

Why have fifty million people moved to the United States since 1820? What makes so many people want to live here?

There are two main reasons. First, people often want to leave their native country if there is no work or if working conditions are poor. Second, people want freedom. If people do not have freedom to do as they wish, they will look for a place to live that has more freedom.

Immigrants come to the United States for better **opportunities**. They hope to find work and get ahead here. America has been rich in iron, coal, forests, and other **natural resources**. We have had lots of materials for manufacturing, which means jobs for people.

The life of an immigrant is not easy, however. It is never easy to leave home and people you care about. Especially when you know you will probably never see them again. It can also be hard to get along in a new country. A big problem may be learning a new language. There are also problems finding work and a place to live. **Natives** may not be *friendly,* either. They may not like people who look and speak differently. •

FREND-lee

From 1820 to 1880, most immigrants came from northern Europe. They were English, Irish, German, and **Scandinavian**. They already spoke English or learned it easily. They became used to America quickly.

Beginning in 1848, Chinese and then Japanese immigrants came, usually to the West Coast. At first, they were *welcomed* because there was a shortage of labor. But later people began to be angry at them because there were fewer jobs to go around. Americans were afraid immigrants would take work away from them.

WEL-kumd

After 1880, most immigrants came from southern and eastern Europe. They were Russians, Poles, Greeks, Slavs, and *Italians*. These new immigrants found it very hard to learn the English language and American customs. It took them a long time to get good jobs and feel at home. •

ih-TAL-yuns

In 1866, 300,000 people came to live in America. That number grew to 789,000 in 1882. Some foreigners arrived here expecting to get rich right away. They had been told that American streets were paved with gold. They found out quickly that this was a dream. Searching for new jobs and for friends from their old country, they usually ended up living in crowded **slums**.

Many Mexican immigrants settled in the Southwest, with most in California. Los Angeles now has a large Mexican population.

Puerto Ricans have also come to the United States in large numbers. Although they are American citizens, many have the same problems of finding good jobs and nice places to live as other immigrants have.

One group of immigrants who did not want to come to America at all were African Blacks. They were brought here against their will, as slaves. Over the years they have had to fight for equality — having the same opportunities and treatment as other Americans. They are still struggling for full equality.

For many years the United States welcomed as many people from other countries as wanted to come. Americans thought immigrants made our country stronger. They had the idea that America was like a "melting pot." People from many different backgrounds could live and work together to make a more interesting, successful country.

In the early 1900s, though, people worried about wages and jobs. They worried and then became angry at foreigners. Congress passed laws that set limits on the number of people we would accept from a country. The number of immigrants went down.

People who are unable to live in their native country because of war or great poverty still come to the United States. For example, many people from the countries in Southeast Asia have come to the United States because the Vietnam War left their countries in ruins. Many immigrants from Latin America, Europe, and Asia try to find work and a better life here.

Immigrants have brought a great deal to the United States. Their hard work has helped develop industries. It has brought this country skilled craftsmen, doctors, artists, and other workers. The different *contributions* of those who have come to this country have made life richer for everyone.

kon-trih-BYOO-shuns

A.

Answer these to review the main ideas.

1. Where did your ancestors come from? How long has your family

   lived in America? _____

_____

2. Why were some Americans unfriendly to immigrants? _____

_____

3. Where did Asian immigrants usually settle? _____

_____

4. Why have immigrants always wanted to come to the United States?

_____

_____

5. Why was it easier for a person from England to immigrate to America

than one from Italy? _____

_____

_____

B.

Circle the right answer to finish each sentence.

1. Since 1820, the total number of immigrants to our country has
   been

   a. one million   b. fifty million   c. forty thousand

2. Between 1820 and 1880, most immigrants came from

   a. northern Europe   b. Africa   c. southern Europe

3. After 1880, most immigrants came from

   a. northern Europe   b. southern Europe   c. South America

4. Immigration today is

   a. as great as it   b. less than it was   c. not allowed
      was in 1900   in 1900

C.

Circle True or False.

T   F   1. Blacks were glad to be immigrants to the United States.

T   F   2. Life has not always been easy for American immigrants.

T   F   3. Immigrants had no skills when they came to America.

T   F   4. Congress made laws to limit immigration.

T   F   5. Without the contributions of immigrants, the United States would
   be a much poorer country.

Choose one of these words to fit each sentence below.

natural resources   opportunity   Scandinavian   slums   natives

1. Finland, Norway, Sweden, Denmark, and Iceland are _____ countries.

2. Many people in American cities have to live in crowded, poor housing called _____.

3. A country with plenty of land, minerals, and forests has good
   _____.

4. We should always be ready to make good use of an _____.

5. _____ are not always friendly to immigrants.

Think about and discuss in class.

Do you dislike people who look different from you or your friends?
Why? _____

_____

_____

Have you ever been disliked by other people because you were different from them? Was there anything you could do about it? _____

_____

_____

Is there as much freedom and opportunity in the United States now as there was in 1870? _____

_____

_____

_____

_____

_____

_____

D.

E.

The American battleship *Maine* was blown up in Havana harbor. This tragedy was one of the events leading to the Spanish-American War.

6

Getting Ready for Chapter Six

Here are six vocabulary words that are used in the story about America becoming a world power. Study these definitions so you will know what each word means when you see it in your reading.

interference   (in-tur-FEER-ents)   Getting involved in other people's business. Getting in the way.

tragedy   (TRA-juh-dee)   Something very sad and terrible, such as sudden death.

enthusiastic   (en-thoo-zee-AS-tik)   Excited and full of energy.

assassinate   (uh-SA-sih-nayt)   Murder an important official, such as a president or a king.

accomplish-ment   (uh-KOM-plish-munt)   Something that has been done, finished. An achievement.

involvement   (in-VOLV-ment)   Taking part in. Joining.

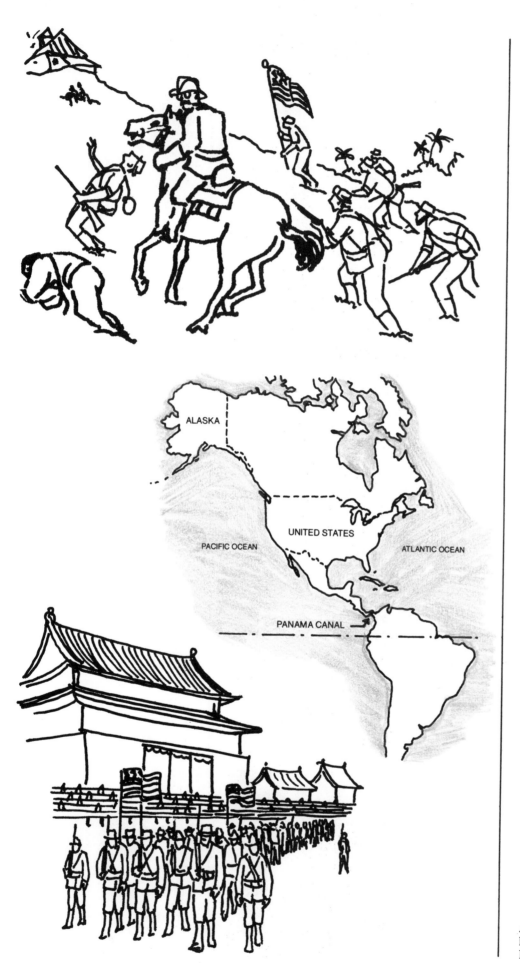

Theodore Roosevelt was a strong supporter of the Spanish-American War. He led an army regiment called the Rough Riders.

The Panama Canal was a short-cut between the Atlantic coast and the Pacific Ocean. A 1978 treaty says that the canal will be neutral and that all ships can use it.

America sent troops to China to help put down the Boxer Rebellion.

America Becomes a World Power

Why did we go to war with Spain?
What kind of a person was Teddy Roosevelt?

Chapter 6

Americans moved around a lot as the country grew. The first settlers built new homes in the wilderness. When that land was developed, people looked for more. As early as 1850 people had their eyes on Cuba. Cuba was rich in sugar, and Southerners wanted to spread slavery there.

In the 1890s the Spanish empire fell apart. In the Americas, Spain still held only Cuba and *Puerto Rico*. Spain's rule in Cuba was cruel. The Spanish rulers took large amounts of money out of the country. People were poor, and there was little freedom. In the Pacific Ocean, the Spanish held the Philippine Islands and Guam. •

por-tuh REE-kow

In 1895 Cuba revolted against Spain. America sympathized with Cuba. We also traded at Cuban ports. In addition, American citizens living in Cuba were badly mistreated by the Spanish. We finally took action because we had a lot of money invested there. We sent the Cubans guns and *ammunition*.

am-yoo-NIH-shun

Spain protested our **interference**. Both sides were becoming angrier. President William McKinley sent the battleship *Maine* to Cuba to protect American citizens and property. One evening in February 1898, the big ship exploded, killing 260 American sailors. No one knows to this day who blew up the *Maine*.

All over the United States, people blamed the **tragedy** on Spain. The newspapers demanded war and revenge. Big newspapers, like those we have today, were just getting started in the late 1800s. The publishers found that the more stories of murder and war they printed, the more papers were sold. People like to read exciting stories, but the newspapers did not always tell the truth.

President McKinley did not want war, but almost everyone in America was screaming for it. McKinley gave in, and war with Spain began in 1898. •

Theodore *Roosevelt* of New York was an eager supporter of the Spanish-American War. "Teddy" Roosevelt was very popular with Americans. He came from a wealthy family and was a *brilliant* student and writer. He had also lived out west and had been a tough cowboy. The best word to describe him is **enthusiastic**.

ROW-zuh-velt

BRIL-yunt

When the war broke out, Teddy Roosevelt was assistant secretary of the Navy in Washington. He had worked to make the United States Navy very strong and ready to fight. It quickly defeated the Spanish fleet.

After he built up the navy, Roosevelt *resigned* his government job and became *colonel* of an army regiment called the Rough Riders. It was made up of eastern college boys and western cowboys — men like Roosevelt himself. The Rough Riders went to Cuba and fought the Spanish army.

ree-ZYND
KER-nul

The Spanish-American War lasted only three months. Spain was badly beaten. She had to turn her empire over to the United States. This included the Philippines, which we wanted as a base to protect our interests in China and Guam.

The United States also took over *Hawaii*, in 1898. Americans had been living there for many years, and we had control of the sugar industry. Now that we owned other islands in the Pacific, Hawaii was more important to us. It gave us good harbors and it was a place where our ships could get fuel on their long voyages to the Philippines. •

huh-WOH-yee

Teddy Roosevelt was vice-president under President McKinley in 1900. The following year, McKinley was **assassinated**, and Roosevelt became president. He was young, he was enthusiastic, and the American people loved him. He seemed like the spirit of America itself.

Roosevelt was famous for quoting the saying "Speak softly and carry a big stick; you will go far." While he was president, the United States was very active in world politics. We sent troops to the Philippines when the people there revolted against American rule. We sent troops to China to help put down the Boxer Rebellion. This was a revolt by the Chinese against foreigners living there. China was very weak at that time and other countries were trying to run her affairs. •

Russia and Japan were at war over the territory of *Manchuria* in 1904. Roosevelt wanted peace in Asia so that Americans could trade there. He called representatives from Japan and Russia to meet with him in New Hampshire. And he stopped the war!

man-CHOOR-ee-uh

In Latin America, Venezuela owed money to Britain, Italy, and Germany, and would not pay it. These countries sent ships to blockade the Venezuelan coast. Roosevelt *persuaded* Britain to back down. He also put *pressure* on Germany to take her case to an international court.

pur-SWAY-dud
PREH-shur

Roosevelt said, however, that we could not allow Europe to use force in the Americas to collect her *debts*. Since we could not let European countries do this, it was up to us to make sure the debts were paid. For example, we sent American troops to the Dominican Republic to make sure they paid European debts. This policy caused us a lot of trouble. Latin Americans did not like our **involvement** in their affairs. In 1930, the U. S. Department of State said officially that we would not use this kind of "police power." •

DETS

Teddy Roosevelt's greatest **accomplishment** was building the Panama Canal. By now, America had business interests all over the world. We needed a canal, a shortcut between the Atlantic coast and the Pacific Ocean. Going around the tip of South America took too long.

Panama was a part of Colombia. However Colombia did not want to give up Panama, which was very important to it. It refused to allow America to take it over.

Suddenly the people of Panama revolted against Colombia. As if by magic, American warships and troops arrived in Panama. They helped Panama keep Colombia from putting down the revolt. Panama then signed a treaty giving the United States the land for the canal. We paid $10 million and a yearly rent.

What had happened? Did Roosevelt pay the people of Panama to revolt against Colombia? No one is absolutely sure. But we do know that Roosevelt said in 1912, "I took Panama. It was the only way the canal could be constructed."

The United States ran the canal until 1978. Then the Senate voted to give Panama control of the canal by the year 2000. The U. S. signed a treaty with Panama. The treaty said the canal will be neutral, and that ships of all nations, including warships, can use it.

Answer these to review the main ideas.

A.

1. Why did the United States go to war with Spain? _____

_____

2. What did Roosevelt mean when he said America should "Speak softly and carry a big stick"? _____

_____

_____

3. What kind of a man was President Theodore Roosevelt? _____

_____

_____

4. How did Teddy Roosevelt arrange to build the Panama Canal?

_____

_____

_____

Circle the right answer to finish each sentence.

B.

1. The battleship *Maine* was sunk by

   a. no one knows   b. Spain   c. Cuba

2. The Spanish-American War lasted

   a. four years   b. one year   c. three months

3. American troops went to China to put down

   a. the Filipino Rebellion   b. the Boxer Rebellion   c. the Japanese

4. Theodore Roosevelt stopped the war between

   a. China and Japan   b. the Philippines and the United States   c. Japan and Russia

Circle True or False.

C.

T   F   1. The Rough Riders were a mixture of eastern college boys and western cowboys.

T   F   2. Teddy Roosevelt believed that our country should keep out of the affairs of other nations.

T   F   3. Hawaii was an important stopping place for American ships sailing to the Philippines.

T   F   4. No one knows just how President Roosevelt arranged to build the Panama Canal.

T   F   5. President McKinley said, "Speak softly and carry a big stick."

Choose one of these words to fit each sentence below.

D.

assassinate   enthusiastic   accomplishment

tragedy   interference   involvement

1. America's _____ in Spain's business in Cuba made the Spanish angry.

2. People get very _____ about their favorite team.

3. If you get an A on this test, that will be an _____!

38

4. Presidents Abraham Lincoln and William McKinley were both
   _____d.

5. A sudden death, like Lincoln's or McKinley's, is a _____.

6. The U.S. had an _____ in Latin-American affairs.

Think about and discuss in class.

"Boxers" is a strange name for the Chinese who took part in the Boxer Rebellion. These Chinese practiced a kind of shadowboxing. That is how they got their name.

Should we Americans keep out of other countries' battles? Or do we have a right to take part? What are the dangers of keeping to ourselves? What are the dangers of being the world's police force?_____

_____

_____

An American statesman said that the Spanish-American War was a "splendid little war." Do you agree? Are any wars "splendid" or good? Do you know of any war you would say was fought for a cause

that was important? _____

_____

_____

How do you think Colombia felt about having Panama taken away

from her? _____

_____

_____

Why is the U.S. willing to give up ownership of the Panama Canal? _____

_____

_____

New and terrible weapons were used in World War I. Among them were airplanes, submarines with torpedoes, machine guns, and poison gas.

Woodrow Wilson was elected president in 1912. He started the League of Nations.

Getting Ready for Chapter Seven

7

Here are four vocabulary words that are used in the story of World War I. Study these definitions so you will know what each word means when you see it in your reading.

underdog   (UN-dur-dog)   Someone who is not expected to win a contest.

blockade   (blah-KAYD)   To use troops or ships to cut off cities and harbors so that they cannot get help from the outside.

torpedo   (tor-PEE-dow)   A large shell containing explosives that can be aimed and fired through the water.

trench   (TRENCH)   A long ditch. A deep, long hole protected by piles of earth that holds soldiers who are in battle.

The First World War

How did we get drawn into World War I?
Why didn't we join the League of Nations?

The nations of Europe were struggling for power in the early 1900s. World War I, the first big war in the 1900s, broke out in 1914. England, France, and Russia, called the Allies, were on one side. Germany, Austria-Hungary, and Turkey were on the other.

President Woodrow Wilson announced that America would be neutral, but from the beginning of the war, we were most sympathetic to the Allies, who were the **underdog**. It seemed to us that Germany was trying to take over Europe. We were worried that they might not stop there.

Germany wanted to send her armies against France. In order to get there, she had to go through *Belgium*, a small country that was neutral. The Belgians did not want any part of the war, but they were in the Germans' way, so they had to defend themselves against invasion. Americans sympathized with the suffering Belgians. They cheered the English and French, who were trying to help Belgium.

BEL-jum

England had a large, well-trained navy. It set up a **blockade** along the German coast, not allowing ships to get by. It was keeping supplies from reaching Germany.

The Germans fought the blockade by using *submarines* to sink ships. Submarines are boats that can go under water. They had just been invented. Without warning, the submarines rose close to the *ocean surface* and launched **torpedoes** at their targets. They hit passenger ships, freighters — anything going to England.

SUB-muh-reenz

OW-shun SUR-fuss

In 1915, a big British passenger ship called the *Lusitania* was sailing off the coast of Ireland. Suddenly, a German submarine closed in on it like a deadly shark. It fired two torpedoes at the *Lusitania*, then disappeared.

loo-sih-TAY-nee-uh

The ship exploded and sank. A total of 1,198 men, women, and children drowned. Of this number, 128 were Americans, mostly women and children. The Germans made no effort to save the passengers. Submarines are too small to rescue any large number of people. Besides, if they come to the surface, warships may see them and blow them to pieces. The American people were very angry. The Germans said they had warned Americans not to sail on British ships.

Months earlier the Germans had announced that any ship trying to trade with the Allies in the waters around the British Isles would be destroyed. President Wilson had warned Germany not to hurt American citizens on Allied ships. He had warned her to leave American ships alone.

The Germans refused. In the next two years more ships were attacked. In 1917 the United States declared war on Germany.

Up to this point, the Germans had been winning the war on land. England and France were holding on desperately. Their ally, Russia, had been crushed and forced to surrender.

American soldiers arrived in France in 1918. The Germans were gaining ground all along the line. World War I was fought from **trenches**. First one side, then the other, would rise out of muddy trenches and charge the enemy. The defenders fired back with machine guns, mowing down soldiers like grass. Millions of people were killed in this terrible war.

With American help, the Allies (England and France) managed to slow the Germans down. Then, as more and more Americans came, the tide turned. Now it was the Allies who broke through the German lines. In 1918, Germany had to surrender. The First World War was over. ●

Woodrow Wilson, unlike Teddy Roosevelt, did not like war. Wilson was really sorry to have to lead his country into World War I. A very *thoughtful* man, Wilson said that the world must form a peace organization. Its members would promise to work together for peace. If any member started a war, the other countries would band together against it. Wilson called this organization the League of Nations.

THOT-fuhl

Most countries joined Wilson's League of Nations. But strangely enough, the United States did not. Many Americans felt that the League could not keep peace without an army of its own. Another reason they opposed the League was that they had been through a war that they thought they might have avoided getting into. They did not want any group made up of other countries to force them to fight a war they didn't want to get involved in.

While it was going on, World War I was a popular cause among the American people. When it was over, however, many people felt differently. They were not happy to have been involved in it.

Answer these to review the main ideas.

A.

1. Why did the United States want the Allies to win the First World War? _____

_____

2. What was the *Lusitania*? _____

What happened to it? _____

_____

3. How were the Allies finally able to defeat the Germans in World War I? _____

_____

4. What was the League of Nations? _____

_____

   Who thought of the idea? _____

   Why didn't the United States join the League of Nations? _____

_____

Circle the right answer to finish each sentence.

B.

1. The First World War started in

   a. 1900   b. 1904   c. 1914

2. To get to France, the Germans sent their armies through

   a. England   b. Belgium   c. Switzerland

3. The United States entered the war in

   a. 1902   b. 1913   c. 1917

4. The Allies were

   a. England, France,   b. Germany   c. neither
      and Russia

5. The United States

   a. joined the League   b. did not join   c. said it would
      of Nations   the League   think about it

6. When the *Lusitania* sank, 1,198 passengers were drowned. The number nearest 1,198 is

   a. 10,000   b. 1,500   c. 1,200

Circle True or False.

C.

T   F   1. World War I was the last world war.

T   F   2. Submarines were invented during the Spanish-American war.

T   F   3. The *Lusitania* was an Italian passenger ship.

T   F   4. If the United States had not entered the war, England and France might have lost.

T F 5. Many Americans felt that if we joined the League of Nations we might have to go to war, even if we didn't want to.

Choose one of these words to fit each sentence below.

D.

torpedo   trench   blockade   underdog

1. If a submarine hits a ship with a _____, the ship will probably sink.

2. If a small college football team plays a big state university, the small college team will be the _____.

3. When ships line up along an enemy coast to keep supplies from getting through, they have made a _____.

4. Soldiers in World War I fought from ditches called _____es.

Think about and discuss in class.

E.

If no one wants war, why do we have so many of them? _____

_____

_____

Since the British Navy was blockading Germany, why wasn't it all right for German submarines to sink British ships? _____

_____

_____

Is there something like a League of Nations in the world today? Does the United States belong? Has it stopped any wars? _____

_____

_____

_____

_____

_____

_____

Henry Ford's assembly-line method of manufacturing produced thousands of cars called the Model T.

Charles Lindbergh made the first non-stop flight across the Atlantic Ocean in 1927 in his plane *The Spirit of St. Louis*.

By 1929, more than one-third of all the homes in the country owned radio sets.

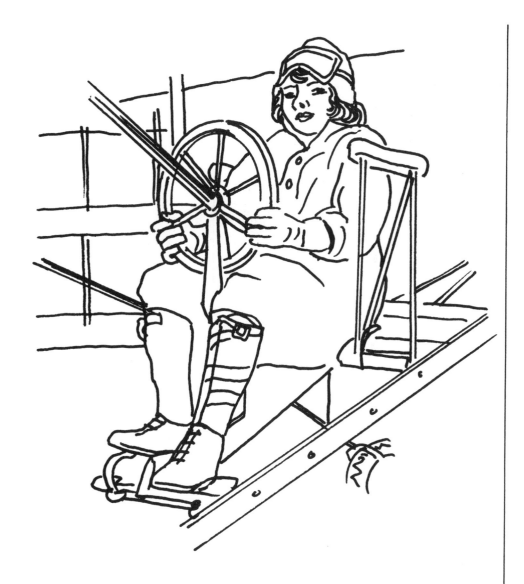

In the twenties, more and more women were doing things women had never done before. This woman is the pilot of an early plane.

Getting Ready for Chapter Eight

8

Here are five vocabulary words that are used in the story of the twenties. Study these definitions so you will know what each word means when you see it in your reading.

ragtime   (RAG-tym)   A kind of lively music with a strong rhythm and beat.

orchestra   (OR-kes-truh)   A group of musicians playing together, usually instruments like violins, clarinets, trumpets, and drums.

audience   (AW-dee-ents)   People watching and listening to a performance; spectators.

prosperity   (prah-SPER-ih-tee)   A time when business is making money and most people are earning a good living.

credit   (KREH-dit)   Buying something and paying for it later. Owing money.

The Twenties

Why were the twenties called the Roaring Twenties?
Women struggled for equal rights in the twenties. What
law helped their cause?
What was the new music of the twenties like?

Chapter

8

In the 1920s in America people wanted to forget about war and hard times. America was growing quickly. It was a time of **prosperity** — of big business, of the growth of cities, and of more money for most Americans.

Henry Ford invented a car called the Model T in 1908. To produce large numbers of cars cheaply, he developed the assembly-line method of manufacturing. An assembly line produces large numbers of things that are exactly alike. Workers use machines made especially for the product. Their work is divided up so that each worker does short, simple tasks over and over.

Using the assembly line, factories produced more *material* goods, which Americans bought in great numbers. Cars, refrigerators, radios, *vacuum* cleaners, and other manufactured products became part of many American households. Many people bought things on **credit**.

muh-TEER-ee-ul

VAK-yoom

Americans had more free time, too. "Talking" movies were invented in 1927, and millions of Americans went to see them. More than half of the American people were living in cities or small towns. Restaurants and dance halls increased. People became interested in *professional* sports like baseball, football, basketball, and hockey.

pruh-FESH-un-ul

Sports stars became popular heroes. In baseball, Babe Ruth, of the New York Yankees, was the leading home-run hitter. In football, a popular hero was Red Grange of Illinois. Grange was called the "Galloping *Ghost*" because he was so hard to tackle. Jack Dempsey was the world *heavyweight* boxing champion. He could hit like a torpedo. In one fight, Dempsey was knocked all the way through the ropes and out of the ring. The people in the **audience** picked him up and threw him back in. Dempsey then knocked out his opponent. •

GOWST
HEH-vee-wayt

The new music of the 1920s was jazz. Jazz developed from the **ragtime** music first played by Black **orchestras** in New Orleans. It was much faster than waltz music. It was good to dance to. It spread north to St. Louis, Chicago and New York.

The "new woman" of the 1900s did not think of herself as weak or helpless. During World War I, while men were fighting, women took their place in factories. Unlike their mothers and grandmothers, these women wore short hair and short skirts. They did this to keep from getting tangled up in the machines they were using.

48

Women also wanted the same political rights as men. In 1920, after a long, hard struggle, they finally won the right to vote. Congress passed the Nineteenth Amendment to the Constitution. It said that "the rights of citizens of the United States to vote shall not be denied or *abridged* by the United States or by any State on account of sex." ●

uh-BRIJD

In 1926, Gertrude *Ederle* swam thirty-five miles across the English Channel from France to England. It took her 14½ hours. A record like this by a woman would have seemed impossible a few years earlier.

EH-dur-lee

A young American named Charles Lindbergh made the first real nonstop airplane flight across the Atlantic Ocean in 1927. His plane was not much more than a box kite, and he had no radio. The "Lone Eagle," as Lindbergh was called, flew by himself from New York to Paris in 33½ hours. The whole world was thrilled by Lindbergh's daring accomplishment. A crowd of 100,000 met him when he landed in Paris. His flight earned him a prize of $25,000.

The Roaring Twenties, as this period is sometimes called, came to a stop in 1929. Business began to decline. Factories closed. Millions of people were thrown out of work. Times got worse and worse. The period of fast growth was over.

Answer these to review the main ideas.

A.

1. Who were some of the sports stars of the 1920s? _____

_____

_____

2. Where did Charles Lindbergh fly? Why was it such an unusual

   trip? _____

_____

3. During World War I, women started to wear short hair and short skirts.

   Why? _____

_____

_____

4. What very important right did women finally win in 1920? _____

_____

_____

5. Where did most Americans live in the twenties? _____

_____

_____

Circle the right answer to finish each sentence.   B.

1. Jack Dempsey was

   a. a football player   b. a boxer   c. a tennis player

2. Gertrude Ederle was

   a. a swimmer   b. a dancer   c. a tennis player

3. In 1920, women won

   a. the right to work   b. the right to strike   c. the right to vote

4. The "Lone Eagle" was

   a. Red Grange   b. Charles   c. Babe Ruth
                              Lindbergh

5. New products were available to

   a. everyone   b. very few   c. most people

Circle True or False.   C.

T   F   1. Times were bad in the 1920s.

T   F   2. Jazz is the same as waltz music.

T   F   3. Gertrude Ederle swam thirty-five miles across the English
           Channel from France to England.

T   F   4. New industries like the automobile industry brought money
           and prosperity to people in the 1920s.

T   F   5. Population stayed the same during the 1920s.

Choose one of these words to fit each sentence below.   D.

orchestra   credit   prosperity

audience   ragtime

1. If you act in a play, you hope it will be watched by a large

   _____.

2. When people have jobs and can buy what they need, it is a time of

    _____.

3. A symphony is played by an _____.

4. Early jazz music with a fast, bouncy beat was called

    _____.

5. If we don't pay for something when we buy it, but pay later, we are

    buying on _____.

Think about and discuss in class.

E.

How long does it take to fly from New York to Paris today? What improvements have been made in airplanes since Lindbergh's time?

_____

_____

_____

How did people spend their leisure time before there were automobiles, movies, TV, and radio? Do you think people are happier

now? _____

_____

Some people think that as long as there are poor Americans, there should be no rich Americans. Do you agree, or do you disagree?

Why? _____

_____

How did the new automobile industry bring prosperity to the United

States in the 1920s? _____

_____

_____

_____

_____

Veterans went to Washington to demand the bonus Congress had promised them. President Hoover ordered the army to use tanks, tear gas, and bayonets to drive them out.

Some people stood on street corners trying to sell apples to earn a bit of money.

A drought in farm states caused dust storms. Crops could not grow. Farmers had to leave and move west.

During the depression millions of Americans were out of work. People had no money for food. They waited in long lines for free food from churches and private charities.

Getting Ready for Chapter Nine

Here are seven vocabulary words that are used in the story about the Great Depression. Study these definitions so you will know what each word means when you see it in your reading.

depression	(dee-PREH-shun) A time when millions of people have no jobs, business is not producing much, and prices are low.
veteran	(VEH-trun) A person who has been in the armed forces and is now out.
bonus	(BOW-nuss) Something extra given in addition to a person's regular pay.
communist	(KOM-you-nist) A person who believes that workers should own and share their nation's wealth. During the twentieth century communist countries were often run by dictators, who opposed freedom and democracy.
drought	(DROUT) A time when there is no rain, and land becomes very dry.
nominate	(NOM-ih-nayt) To choose a candidate to run for office.
energetic	(en-ur-JEH-tik) Active, eager, and busy. Full of force and power.

The Great Depression

Why did factories close?
What did the veterans want?
Did Herbert Hoover help cut down unemployment?

Chapter 9

"Brother, can you spare a dime?" was a popular song in the 1930s. Millions of Americans were out of work. Every day more banks lost their money and closed. Factories closed. People who had invested, or put money in businesses, lost their savings. People spent long hours in lines waiting for free food. Families lost their homes. Some people stood on street corners trying to sell apples at five cents each. Others simply begged for a nickel or a dime.

Why was this **depression** happening? It is a hard question, with many possible answers, but we do know a few reasons. We had been producing a great deal — more things than we could use. A few big *corporations* had most of the country's wealth and power. Most people were not earning enough money to live on.

kor-por-AY-shuns

Foreign countries were having problems of their own, and were buying fewer and fewer American goods. More and more buying was being done on credit. Both our government and *individuals* were in debt. •

in-dih-VID-yoo-ulz

Herbert Hoover, a Republican, was the president of the United States. Hoover had strong beliefs. He believed that people should look after themselves. They should not depend on the government to help them. He thought that those in need could get help from charities like the Salvation Army or church organizations. He couldn't believe that there were as many as twelve million people out of work.

Hoover tried to help. He reduced taxes and made some government loans to business people and farmers. But it was not enough. The depression continued. In January 1933, one out of three American workers was out of a job, and many of those who did have jobs were getting very low wages. There were nearly thirteen million unemployed.

In 1932, an "army" of about fourteen thousand World War I **veterans** gathered in Washington, D.C. They demanded that Congress give them their **bonus,** or extra money, for having served in the war. They said they were too poor to wait until 1945, when the bonus was to be paid to them. They built shacks to live in out of boards and packing boxes. This was called the veterans' camp.

Congress refused to pay the men a bonus. President Hoover said that some of the veterans were criminals or **communists**. He ordered them to leave Washington. Some did leave, but most stayed. Then Hoover called out the United States Army. The army used tanks and tear gas to drive the veterans out. Under General Douglas MacArthur, cavalry troops rode through the camp, swinging their swords at the veterans. Other soldiers carried bayonets. They threw tear-gas bombs at the campers. Fires broke out. Within a few minutes, the veterans fled. The "Bonus March" was over, but people remembered it. •

Farmers were suffering, too. There was a heat wave and a **drought** in the farm states. Crops failed. The lack of water turned the dry soil to dust. Then powerful winds blew the dust away.

In Oklahoma, the farmers had nothing left to farm. Thousands of "Okies," as they were called, piled into worn-out cars and trucks. They headed west to California, hoping to find work there. Many of the cars broke down, and their *passengers* never reached California. Those who managed to get there looked for jobs picking fruit. These jobs were *scarce*, too.

PASS-un-jurs

SKAYRS

During the depression communists talked about the need for revolution in the United States, but most Americans didn't agree with them. Americans continued to express their feelings with their votes.

Hoover ran for president again in 1932. He blamed the depression on conditions all over the world. And indeed, many other countries were as badly off as the United States. Hoover also had harsh words for the Democrats. He thought their programs would not help business. He warned that if the Democrats won, "Grass will grow in the streets of a hundred cities, a thousand towns."

The Democrats **nominated** Franklin Delano Roosevelt, governor of New York, for president. Roosevelt was a distant cousin of Teddy Roosevelt, and also very rich and **energetic**. FDR, as he was called, had been disabled by a *disease* called *polio*. His legs were paralyzed, and he could not walk alone.

dih-ZEEZ   PO-lee-o

Even though he was in a wheelchair, Roosevelt traveled all over the country to ask for people's votes. He offered Americans a "New Deal." Government and business would work together to help the country get over the depression. He said he would
(1) find work for those who were unemployed;
(2) help the farmers;
(3) build up the railroads;
(4) protect those in need; and
(5) reduce government spending.

The American people liked Roosevelt's promises more than they liked Hoover's warnings. In 1932 most voters chose Roosevelt. It was now up to Roosevelt and the Democrats to lead the country out of the Great Depression.

Answer these to review the main ideas. A.

1. How did President Hoover feel about helping people during the Great Depression? _____

   _____

   _____

2. What did Hoover do to try to end the depression? _____

   _____

   _____

3. What happened to the veterans who asked Congress for a bonus?

   _____

   _____

4. Who were the "Okies"? Why did they go to California? _____

   _____

   _____

5. Who won the presidential election in 1932? _____

   _____

Circle True or False. B.

T F 1. President Herbert Hoover was a Republican.

T F 2. Hoover said that needy Americans could rely on the government for aid.

T F 3. In January 1933, one out of every three Americans was out of a job.

T F 4. The veterans were rewarded with a large bonus.

Circle the right answer to finish each sentence. C.

1. In 1933, the number of unemployed persons in America was nearly

   a. ten thousand   b. thirteen million   c. ten million

2. The United States Army

   a. fed and clothed the veterans   b. helped the veterans build their camp   c. drove the veterans out of Washington, D.C.

56

3. A state especially hard hit by dust storms was

   a. Oklahoma   b. California   c. Connecticut

4. "Grass will grow in the streets of a hundred cities, a thousand towns," was said by

   a. Herbert Hoover   b. Franklin   c. Theodore
                            Roosevelt   Roosevelt

Choose one of these words to fit each sentence below.   **D.**

   energetic   bonus   communist

   drought   depression   veteran

   nominate

1. When there is no rain and the land dries up, there is a

   _____.

2. Servicemen and women who have left the armed forces are

   called _____s.

3. Those who favor a revolution so that the workers can share the

   wealth are _____s.

4. Herbert Hoover was _____d for a second term as

   president, but lost the election.

5. Americans went through very hard times during the

   _____.

6. Good workers often get a _____ along with their
   salary at Christmas.

7. A person who gets up at five in the morning and does exercises is

   _____.

Think about and discuss in class.   **E.**

Whom do you think the veterans of the march on Washington voted for

in 1932? Why? _____

_____

_____

What did President Hoover mean when he said that if the Democrats won, grass would grow in the streets of our cities and towns? Did it?

_____

_____

What would Herbert Hoover think of the many welfare programs our government has today? What would he advise us to do instead? _____

_____

_____

_____

What can be done to prevent droughts and dust storms like the one in the 1930s? _____

_____

_____

_____

President Franklin Roosevelt acted right away to fight the depression. The government spent billions of dollars to create jobs and programs for people in need.

Getting Ready for Chapter Ten

10

Here are seven vocabulary words that are used in the story about the New Deal. Study these definitions so you will know what each word means when you see it in your reading.

frantic	(FRAN-tik)	Frightened and desperate.
revive	(ree-VIVE)	Bring back to life or consciousness.
agency	(AY-jen-see)	A business or service that acts for others.
administration	(ad-min-ih-STRAY-shun)	A group of people who manage a business or project. Management.
civilian	(sih-VIL-yun)	Anyone who is not in the armed forces.
conservation	(kon-ser-VAY-shun)	Saving and caring for something. Protecting forests, rivers, minerals, coal, gas, oil, and other natural resources.
budget	(BUD-jet)	A list of what is earned and what is spent. A plan for using money.

The WPA hired people to build schools, highways, airports, playgrounds, and dams.

Many farmers could not make a living and had to sell their farms. The Agricultural Adjustment Act paid farmers *not* to produce.

The New Deal

What was the New Deal?
Why did businesses oppose it?
What was the brain trust?

President Franklin D. Roosevelt was a man of action. He was ready to try anything that might help cure the Great Depression.

Roosevelt was inaugurated as president on March 4, 1933. On that day, banks all over the country were closed. People were **frantic**. Some people were afraid they might lose all the savings they had put into the banks. Millions of people still had no jobs.

President Roosevelt was calm and *encouraging*. Talking on the radio, he said "This is . . . the time to speak the truth . . . frankly and boldly . . . This great nation will . . . **revive** and prosper . . . The only thing we have to fear is fear itself."

en-KUH-rij-ing

Roosevelt quickly asked Congress to pass a law that reopened the banks. The law also gave the *Treasury* the power to print money. This brought relief to a frightened nation. •

TREH-zhoo-ree

Herbert Hoover had been afraid to spend government money to help the people. He thought it was un-American and un-businesslike. Hoover's government had made loans, but expected the money to be paid back.

Roosevelt was completely different. When he was president, the government spent billions of dollars, giving help to people in need. At times, it spent more money than it took in from taxpayers.

The Federal *Emergency* Relief Act gave money to states, cities, and towns. **Agencies** to help the needy and unemployed were started. One was the WPA (Works Progress **Administration**). The WPA hired people to build schools, highways, airports, playgrounds, and dams. Another agency was the CCC (**Civilian Conservation** *Corps*). It gave jobs to young men who liked to work outdoors. The men camped out and planted trees, built dams, and finished other useful jobs.

ee-MUR-jun-see

KOR

The *Social Security* Act was passed in 1935. This program gives workers unemployment insurance — regular payments when they are out of work. In addition, it says that when workers retire, they can get monthly payments when they are sixty-five. Part of the money for this program comes from the federal government, and part from the states. The workers themselves, and their employers, also contribute to the program.

SOW-shul seh-KYOOR-ih-tee

Roosevelt helped farmers, too. For years they had raised more crops and livestock than they could sell. Prices were very low. Farmers almost had to give away what they had raised.

What could be done for the farmers? If there were fewer crops and livestock on sale at the market, prices would go up. People are willing to pay more for items that are hard to get.

Roosevelt persuaded Congress to pass a very unusual law. The *Agricultural* Adjustment Act told farmers to plant less grain, cotton, tobacco, peanuts, and sugar. Farmers were paid *not* to produce so much. Cotton crops were destroyed. Six million pigs were killed. The pork was frozen and over 100 million pounds of it were given to families who needed food. Prices on cotton and pigs rose. The farmers received more money. •

ag-rih-KUL-choor-ul

President Roosevelt continued his experiments. He had a group of college professors to advise him what to try next to get the country moving again. These advisors were called his "brain trust."

Businesses were angry at Roosevelt because they said he was spending too much money. ''That's no way to run things,'' they said. ''The government should have a 'balanced **budget**.' It should not spend more than it takes in. If it keeps on printing money, the money will become worthless. The country will be ruined.''

The New Deal had an answer. ''People are more important than money. Millions of Americans need jobs. It's up to the government to help them.'' President Roosevelt believed that creating jobs for people would make the country well again. If the government helped people find jobs, they would be able to buy more goods. Stores and factories would reopen. They would sell more and be able to hire more workers. The country would recover from the depression. •

Most business people hated Roosevelt and his brain trust. They did not think the government should make so many new rules and policies. They thought Roosevelt was a madman and a dictator. In turn, Roosevelt disliked them. He thought their greed had almost ruined the country. The New Deal had helped get people as well as businesses back on their feet. Now that the worst was over, the businesses were complaining.

Most Americans, however, supported Roosevelt. He had done them far more good than harm. They reelected him president in 1936, 1940, and 1944. No other president has ever been elected four times, and probably none will. It is now against the law to serve more than two terms.

How successful was the New Deal? The relief programs of the New Deal helped people believe in their government again. But the jobs the government created helped only a small number of all the people who needed help. In addition, the pay for these jobs was often low. From 1933 to 1936 the economy got only a little better. But Roosevelt tried his best to end the Great Depression. Like his cousin Teddy, Franklin Roosevelt was a bold leader of the people.

Answer these to review the main ideas.

1. What was America like when Franklin Roosevelt became president

   in 1933? _____

   _____

   _____

2. What was the difference between the ideas of Herbert Hoover and

   Franklin Roosevelt? _____

   _____

   _____

3. How did President Roosevelt reduce unemployment? _____

   _____

   _____

   _____

4. What is the Social Security program? _____

   _____

   _____

5. What did business people think of Roosevelt? What did Roosevelt

   think of them?_____

   _____

   _____

6. How successful was the New Deal? _____

   _____

   _____

Circle the right answer to finish each sentence below.

1. Franklin Roosevelt became president of the United States in

   a. 1903   b. 1933   c. 1973

2. The CCC gave jobs to

   a. young men   b. old men   c. women

3. The New Deal told the farmers to

   a. produce more   b. produce less   c. produce the
      crops and livestock   same amount
                                               as usual

4. President Roosevelt had a group of advisers called

   a. the WPA   b. the brain trust   c. the CCC

5. Roosevelt was elected president

   a. twice   b. once   c. four times

Circle True or False.

C.

T   F   1. Most business people liked President Roosevelt.

T   F   2. Herbert Hoover said, "The only thing we have to fear is fear
           itself."

T   F   3. President Roosevelt thought that giving jobs to people
           would help the country recover.

T   F   4. The Social Security program ended many years ago.

T   F   5. Farm prices went up after farmers destroyed some of their
           crops and killed their pigs.

Choose one of these words to fit each sentence below.

D.

civilian   conservation   administration

agency   revive   budget

frantic

1. A good _____ will run a program smoothly.

2. Now we must practice _____ of our energy and

   resources.

3. If we become tired and worried, we should try to _____
   our spirits.

4. If people don't make much money, they must live on a tight

   _____.

5. Swimmers who are afraid of drowning may become _____.

6. After the war, the soldier became a _____ again.

7. A business or service which acts for others is an _____ .

Think about and discuss in class.

During the New Deal, Congress passed hundreds of laws. One of them set up a business called the Tennessee Valley Authority (TVA) in the South. The TVA built dams and electric power plants along the rivers. It sold electric power to factories at very low prices. The government could do this because it did not need to make a profit. Private power companies in the South could not sell power as cheaply as the TVA. Their business was hurt. If you had been working for a private power company then, what would you have thought of the New Deal and the TVA? Should the government help people or business? Can it do both?

_____

_____

_____

The United States Supreme Court threatened the New Deal. It ruled that many New Deal laws were unconstitutional. They were no longer laws. President Roosevelt was furious. He said he would replace the justices with people who were sympathetic to his ideas. Most Americans thought F.D.R.'s plan to appoint new justices was a very bad idea. Can you think of some reasons why?

_____

_____

Adolf Hitler started the Nazi Party. He thought Jews were inferior and should be destroyed. Six million European Jews were murdered during the Second World War.

EUROPE IN WORLD WAR II

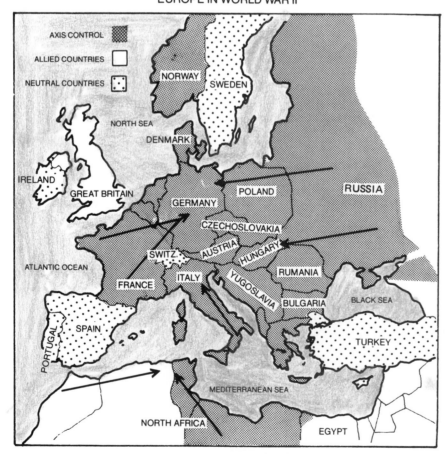

AXIS CONTROL

ALLIED COUNTRIES

NEUTRAL COUNTRIES

NORWAY
SWEDEN
NORTH SEA
DENMARK
IRELAND
GREAT BRITAIN
GERMANY
POLAND
RUSSIA
CZECHOSLOVAKIA
SWITZ.
AUSTRIA
HUNGARY
ATLANTIC OCEAN
FRANCE
ITALY
YUGOSLAVIA
RUMANIA
BULGARIA
BLACK SEA
PORTUGAL
SPAIN
TURKEY
MEDITERRANEAN SEA
NORTH AFRICA
EGYPT

Russian soldiers pushed against Germany from the East; Americans and British stormed through Italy and France from the South and the West. The Germans surrendered in 1945.

American and British soldiers landed on the coast of France in June 1944. Heavy tank forces defeated the Germans there.

Getting Ready for Chapter Eleven

11

Here are four vocabulary words that are used in the story about the Second World War. Study these definitions so you will know what each word means when you see it in your reading.

concentration camp (kon-sen-TRAY-shun KAMP)   A special prison where a government puts its enemies.

horrified (HAR-ih-fide)   Shocked. Terrified and frightened.

atomic bomb (a-TOM-ik BOM)   A bomb whose power comes from the splitting of atoms. Atoms are the smallest bits or building blocks in nature.

radiation (ray-dee-AY-shun)   Energy in the form of waves or particles given out as a result of a nuclear explosion or other things like x-rays.

The Second World War

Who was Adolf Hitler?

Why did we drop the atomic bomb?

World War II began in Europe in 1939. England and France were lined up against Germany. Germany and Italy had been piling up lots of guns. They were beginning to take over territories near them. America did not want to get into another war in Europe. But Germany was very powerful. America began to worry.

A dictator named Adolf Hitler had come to power in Germany. Hitler had fought in the First World War. He was angry that Germany had lost in 1918. He wanted to conquer new territory in Europe to make Germany a big power, and he wanted to be the ruler.

Hitler started the *Nazi* Party. The Nazis believed that the white German people were the one perfect "master race." They thought all other people were inferior. They especially hated the Jews. Hitler believed the Jews were inferior, and therefore, they must be destroyed. He forced them into **concentration camps**, where they were *tortured* and killed. Six million European Jews were murdered during the Second World War. •

The Nazis invaded Austria and *Czechoslovakia* and put them under German rule. They also took over Poland, Denmark, and Norway. In 1940, they invaded Holland and Belgium and conquered France.

Then the Germans prepared to invade England. Nazi planes bombed London and other British cities. Tens of thousands of British citizens were killed or injured. However, under Prime Minister Winston Churchill, the English held on and fought back with their own planes.

Most Americans were **horrified** at what was happening. Italy and Japan were allied with Germany. These three nations called themselves the Axis powers. They were all ruled by dictators who wanted to conquer other countries and increase their own power.

President Franklin Roosevelt believed that the Axis powers threatened the United States. Germany might conquer all of Europe. Japan might take over Asia. If that happened, what would these countries do next? •

Suddenly Germany *launched* a surprise attack on the Soviet Union.* The Soviet Union was a communist country whose ruler was Joseph Stalin. Because the Soviet Union was a communist country we were not allies, but we helped them anyway. We sent guns, tanks, and planes to both the Soviet Union and England because they were fighting Hitler's Germany. We also prepared to defend our own country from an attack by the Axis powers.

NAH-tsee

TOR-choord

cheh-kow-slow-VAH-kee-uh

LONCHT

*In 1922 the Union of Soviet Socialist Republics (U.S.S.R.), or Soviet Union for short, became the correct name for the country formerly known as Russia. However, the use of the names Russia and Russians for all of the Soviet Union and its people continued until recently because the Russian Republic was the largest in the nation.

Then on December 7, 1941, disaster struck. Without any warning, Japanese ships and planes attacked the American base at Pearl Harbor, Hawaii. A large part of our navy was sunk.

Panic hit the United States. People feared that the Japanese army would cross the Pacific Ocean to invade California and that the many Japanese-Americans living on the West Coast would help Japan.

In 1942, the American government unfairly rounded up 120,000 Americans of Japanese descent and shipped them inland to special camps. Innocent men, women, and children were forced to live behind barbed wire, guarded by soldiers. Most of the victims, who had to give up their homes and jobs with little warning, were loyal American citizens. •

After Pearl Harbor, the United States went to war with the Axis powers. In Europe, our armies fighting against Germany were commanded by General Dwight D. *Eisenhower*. General Douglas MacArthur commanded those fighting against Japan in Asia.

EYE-zen-how-ur

Our war plan was to try to defeat Germany first. From England, American and British troops stormed on to the beaches of France in June 1944. They drove through France and into Germany itself. The Allied soldiers also invaded Italy and captured Rome.

Meanwhile, the Russians pushed against Germany from the East. They, too, entered Germany. In 1945, the Americans and Russians met near Berlin, the German capital. Adolf Hitler killed himself, and Germany surrendered. •

Now it was Japan's turn to be attacked. American forces fought their way to Japan over a large number of islands in the Pacific. They captured the Philippines, Okinawa, and *Iwo Jima*. Other Americans helped drive the Japanese out of China. American airplanes battered Japanese cities into flaming ruins. The United States warned Japan to surrender, but the Japanese refused.

ee-wow JEE-muh

On August 6, 1945, an American plane flew over the city of Hiroshima, Japan. The plane dropped a secret new bomb on the city. It was an **atomic bomb**, the most powerful weapon that had been invented up to that time. The atomic bomb destroyed Hiroshima. Only a few buildings remained. Over 71,000 Japanese men, women, and children died in the smoke and flames. About 130,000 more died later because of the **radiation** from the explosion. When Japan *still* refused to surrender, another atomic bomb was dropped on the city of Nagasaki. Almost half of Nagasaki's buildings were destroyed, and 74,000 more people were killed.

That was the end of World War II. The frightful atomic bomb left no hope for Japan. Japan surrendered to General MacArthur on board the United States battleship *Missouri* in *Tokyo* Bay. The date was September 2, 1945.

TOW-kee-yow

Answer these to review the main ideas.

A.

1. What kind of a person was Adolf Hitler? _____

_____

2. What happened to France in 1940? _____

_____

_____

3. Why did the United States send war supplies to the Soviet Union?

_____

_____

4. How did the United States get into World War II? _____

_____

_____

5. How did World War II end? _____

_____

_____

Circle True or False.

B.

T F 1. Nazi Germany put six million European Jews to death in World War II.

T F 2. Germany defeated England and France in World War II.

T F 3. The American government forced 120,000 Japanese-Americans to live in camps, guarded by soldiers.

T F 4. General Dwight Eisenhower and General Douglas MacArthur commanded American soldiers in the Second World War.

T F 5. America's war plan was to defeat Japan first, and then to fight Germany.

Circle the right answer to finish each sentence.

C.

1. Adolf Hitler called the Germans

   a. peaceful   b. the "master race"   c. the "friendly race"

2. Hitler especially hated

    a. the English   b. the Jews   c. Christians

3. The Prime Minister of England was

    a. Franklin   b. Joseph Stalin   c. Winston
       Roosevelt   Churchill

4. Germany, Italy, and Japan called themselves

D.

    a. the Axis Powers   b. the Allies   c. the Central
                                           Powers

5. At the end of World War II, Hitler

    a. became a prisoner   b. killed himself   c. became president
                                            of Germany

6. The first city hit by an atomic bomb was

    a. London, England   b. Paris, France   c. Hiroshima, Japan

Choose one of these words to fit each sentence below.

D.

    concentration camp   atomic bomb   radiation   horrified

1. The _____ from an atomic bomb can be as dangerous
    as the bomb itself.

2. If you lived in a country ruled by a dictator, and you were against

    the government, you might be put in a _____.

3. A single _____ can destroy a whole city.

4. People were _____ when they learned what Hitler was
    doing.

Think about and discuss in class.

E.

Adolf Hitler boasted that the Germans were the best people on earth.
Are some people or countries *better* than others? How or why? How

can you tell? _____

_____

_____

_____

The Soviets tried to get control of West Berlin. They closed off all roads to the city. American cargo planes made an airlift to bring supplies to the people.

THE COLD WAR — 1947

ICELAND

FINLAND

NORWAY

SWEDEN

DENMARK

IRELAND

SOVIET UNION

GT. BRITAIN

HOLLAND
WEST GERMANY   Berlin
BELGIUM   POLAND
LUX.   EAST GERMANY

CZECHOSLOVAKIA

FRANCE

AUSTRIA

SWITZ.   HUNGARY

ITALY   RUMANIA

PORTUGAL   YUGOSLAVIA

SPAIN   BULGARIA

ALBANIA

TURKEY

GREECE

COUNTRIES RECEIVING HELP FROM
U.S. UNDER MARSHALL PLAN

COUNTRIES DOMINATED BY THE SOVIET UNION

In the Cold War, the Soviet Union tried to spread communism in Europe by encouraging revolutions. America tried to stop this by sending money to help these countries recover from World War II.

The United Nations works to prevent war. Does it succeed?

Getting Ready for Chapter Twelve

12

Here are six vocabulary words that are used in the story of the Cold War. Study these definitions so you will know what each word means when you see it in your reading.

headquarters (HED-kwor-terz) The main office. The place from which orders are sent.

satellite (SAT-uh-lyt) A smaller body that circles around a larger body. The moon is a satellite of the earth. Countries controlled by larger countries are also called satellites.

guerrillas (guh-RIH-luz) Armed men and women (not always soldiers) who make daring raids behind enemy lines, and who are not part of a regular army.

airlift (AIR-lift) A way of carrying soldiers or supplies by air when land routes are blocked.

cargo (KAR-gow) Freight carried by an airplane, ship, or other means of transportation.

triumph (TRY-umf) Victory; success.

The Cold War

Who fought in the Cold War ?
What was the "Iron Curtain"?

After two world wars, people everywhere hoped that peace would last. The old League of Nations was dead. In its place was a new organization called the United Nations.

At the end of World War I, our country refused to join the League of Nations. We wanted to be left alone. However, after World War II, Americans thought it was important to work for peace with other nations. The United States was the first country to join the United Nations in 1945. **Headquarters** of the UN is now in New York City. In 1991, 166 countries were members.

The UN ran into trouble from the beginning. The United States and the Soviet Union could not get along together. The United States said that the people of Europe should be free and have democratic government. Most Europeans agreed.

The Soviets, however, supported the communist activities in Europe. Stalin wanted European communists to rise up and overthrow their governments. The Soviets wanted to use eastern Europe as protection in case of attacks from the west. They would help their fellow communists in any way they could. •

This struggle between the United States and the Soviet Union is called the Cold War. The world's two strongest powers did not fight each other with guns, as in a "hot" war. Instead, the Soviet Union tried to spread communism by encouraging revolutions. The United States was opposed to communism and tried to stop it from spreading.

The United Nations could do nothing to stop the Cold War. The UN stood aside while the United States and the Soviet Union argued and quarreled.

After the end of World War II, Germany was divided into two big parts, East and West. The Soviets occupied the East. The U.S., England, and France divided up the West. The Soviets set up a communist government in East Germany. In addition, Stalin wanted all the countries bordering on the Soviet Union to be communist. The Soviet Union set about to control Poland, Hungary, and other countries in Eastern Europe. These countries did not succeed in keeping the Soviets out. Soviet tanks rolled through their streets. Communists were in charge of their governments. These countries became **satellites** of the Soviet Union. •

Prime Minister Winston Churchill of England warned of what was happening. He said the Soviets were bringing down an "iron curtain" across Europe. Behind that curtain the Soviets were in control. People there were living under communism and had no freedom. The states took their orders from Stalin.

Chapter 12

The Soviet Union supported the communist **guerrillas** in a civil war against the government of Greece. It also put pressure on Turkey. In 1947, President Harry Truman, of the United States, sent money and military supplies to those two countries. Truman promised to help any nation that did not want to be taken over by communists. This promise was called the Truman *Doctrine*. It stopped communism in Turkey and Greece.

DOK-trin

In 1947, our Secretary of State, George C. Marshall, suggested another plan to stop communism. Western Europe had been badly damaged in World War II. Cities and factories had been destroyed. People were without jobs. Some were so discouraged that they were ready to turn to communism.

Under the Marshall Plan, the United States spent billions of dollars rebuilding Western Europe. Sixteen nations, including England, France, Italy, and West Germany, got American help. Western Europe recovered from the war and remained anti-communist. •

Berlin, the capital of Germany, was inside East Germany. East Germany was controlled by the Soviets, as you know. Because Berlin was such an important city, its government was divided into zones, too. American soldiers were stationed in Berlin.

The communists hoped to get control of the allied zones. They ordered the Americans to leave Berlin. They closed off all roads to the city. It looked as if the western part of Berlin, the part that the Americans held, would be starved out. Over two million Germans lived in West Berlin.

Instead of leaving Berlin, the Americans started an **airlift**. Hundreds of American **cargo** airplanes flew to West Berlin daily. For almost a year they brought in food and coal for the people there. There was nothing the communists could do unless they wanted a big war. Neither side was ready for that. So the Soviet Union backed down, and the Americans stayed in West Berlin. The airlift was a great **triumph**.

In the Cold War, the United States was able to keep Western Europe from becoming communist. But in Asia, the communists were successful in a revolution in 1949 in the huge country of China. America was worried about Asia. The next chapter will tell about something that happened there.

Answer these to review the main ideas.

A.

1. What was the cause of big problems in the United Nations? _____

_____

_____

2. What was the Cold War? _____

_____

3. Why did the Soviet Union want Eastern Europe especially to be

communist? _____

_____

4. How did the United States fight communism in Western Europe?

_____

_____

5. How did the United States save West Berlin? _____

_____

Match the dates in the first column with the events in the second column. Draw a line between each date and the event.

B.

1945   China taken over by Communists.

1947   Berlin airlift saves West Berlin.

1947   United States joins United Nations.

1948   Truman Doctrine helps Greece and Turkey.

1949   Marshall Plan helps Western Europe.

Circle True or False.

C.

T F 1. The United States joined the League of Nations at the end of World War I.

T F 2. A "cold war" is a shorter war than a "hot war."

T F 3. The Soviet Union wanted communism to spread all over the world.

T F 4. The "iron curtain" was the idea of President Truman.

Circle the right answer to finish each sentence.

D.

1. The first country to join the United Nations was

    a. the United States   b. the Soviet Union   c. Germany

2. President Truman's promise to help other nations fight communism was called

    a. the Truman   b. the iron curtain   c. the United
       Doctrine   Nations

3. Stalin's way of fighting the Cold War was to

   a. drop atomic   b. use the navy   c. encourage
      bombs   communist
                                                revolutions

4. The Berlin airlift was

   a. a great triumph   b. a Soviet victory   c. a West German
      for America   defeat

Choose one of these words to fit each sentence below.

E.

cargo   satellite   headquarters

guerrillas   triumph   airlift

1. The United States used an _____ to feed the people
   of West Berlin.

2. An object that revolves or circles around a larger object is a

   _____.

3. A great victory is the same as a great _____.

4. In business, or in the armed forces, the main office is called

   _____.

5. Goods carried by ships or airplanes from one place to another are

   called _____.

6. _____ were fighting in the villages of Greece.

Think about and discuss in class.

F.

After their revolution in 1917 the Soviet government owned most property and businesses and controlled the press. There was little individual freedom, in the sense that we know it in the West, but there was also almost no unemployment.

By 1990, though, under the leadership of Mikhail Gorbachev, who was the premier, the Soviet Union moved quickly away from communism and a lot of government control to a system more like those in the West. More businesses were owned privately and organized to make a profit. Things people could buy became more important, and people had more individual freedom. Other countries in eastern Europe that had been communist also changed, moving toward Western democracy. Surprisingly, the Cold War was over.

In what way do you think the end of the Cold War between East and West affected everyone in the world? _____

How do you think the change from communism to capitalism might affect a family in eastern Europe? What improvements in their lives might take place? Can you think of anything that might *not* be an improvement?

The two parts of Korea fought in the Korean War. The North was helped by the Soviet Union and China. The United States and its allies helped South Korea.

Getting Ready for Chapter Thirteen

13

Here are five vocabulary words that are used in the story about the war in Korea. Study these definitions so you will know what each word means when you see it in your reading.

peninsula   (pen-IN-suh-luh)   A piece of land reaching out into the water and almost surrounded by it.

equipment   (ee-KWIP-ment)   Goods and supplies. For soldiers this includes weapons, uniforms, and tools.

crisis   (KRY-siss)   A turning point; a time of great importance which may decide whether things will stay the same, get better, or get worse.

truce   (TROOS)   An agreement to stop fighting; a pause during a war for peace talks.

polls   (POLES)   A place where people vote.

General Douglas MacArthur thought bombing China would end the war. His commander-in-chief, President Truman, said no. He was afraid that might start World War III.

Soldiers from several countries fought in the United Nations forces in Korea.

The War in Korea

Who fought against the communist forces in Korea?
Why did President Truman fire General MacArthur?

In 1950 the Cold War turned hot. Communist forces in Asia tried to take over a small country called Korea.

Korea lies on a **peninsula** off the coast of Asia. It is a next-door neighbor of China. After World War II ended in 1945, Korea was divided into two parts. These were North Korea and South Korea. The North Koreans were communists. They received help from the Soviet Union and China. The South Koreans were against communism. They were helped by the United States and its allies.

In June 1950, North Korean armies invaded South Korea. The United States rushed troops to help the South Koreans. We also called on the United Nations members for aid. One of the duties of the UN is to put down small wars before they become large.

The United Nations agreed to help. It named General Douglas MacArthur of the United States commander of the UN forces. United Nations members sent troops, too. England, Canada, *Australia*, France, Greece, and Turkey all helped. But most UN soldiers were South Koreans and Americans.•

aw-STRAY-lyuh

The North Korean army had been well trained by the Soviet Union. It had Soviet **equipment**. At first the communist forces won one battle after another. But General MacArthur suddenly launched a surprise attack behind their lines. The North Koreans were trapped. They were pushed back into North Korea all the way to the Chinese border. It looked as if the UN had won the war.

But the Chinese surprised the allies when they entered the war. Perhaps the Soviets asked them to attack. Perhaps the Chinese were afraid the Americans would invade China. In any case, a million Chinese soldiers charged into North Korea. They pushed the United Nations back to South Korea. There the UN soldiers were finally able to hold.

General MacArthur was furious. He had been a great hero in both world wars. Now he was being beaten. MacArthur asked President Truman to send planes to bomb China. He also needed more troops. MacArthur said, "We must win. There is no *substitute* for victory."

SUB-stih-toot

This war was really a United Nations war, however, not just a U.S. war. Many of our allies in the UN, especially Britain, were against spreading the war to China. Other American generals also opposed it. Truman, too, thought it would be a mistake to start a war with China. The Soviet Union might use atomic bombs in China's defense, and that might start World War III. The whole earth might be destroyed in an atomic war.

Truman told MacArthur to do the best he could with the soldiers he had. He told him to defend South Korea *only*. He did not want to do anything to start a third world war.

MacArthur was still angry. He did not want to obey the orders of the UN or of Truman, his commander-in-chief. Finally, Mr. Truman removed MacArthur from his job. "I could do nothing else and still be president of the United States," Truman explained.

MacArthur returned to the United States. Many people hailed him as a hero who hadn't been given a fair chance. But the country also gained respect for President Truman. He had kept calm during a **crisis**.

After MacArthur left, the war slowed down. The armies fought each other along the line that divided North and South Korea. In 1951, representatives of the communists and the United Nations began **truce** talks. Small battles continued off and on, however. The war was not yet really over. •

In 1952, Americans went to the **polls** to elect a new president. Truman had been in office eight years and did not want to run again. The Democrats' nominee for president was Governor Adlai Stevenson, of Illinois. The Republicans nominated General Dwight Eisenhower for president. Eisenhower had commanded our winning armies in Europe in World War II.

Eisenhower blamed the Truman administration for the fact that the war was not over yet. He promised that if he were elected, he would go to Korea and do what he could to end the war. Eisenhower was very popular with his fellow citizens. The American people believed he could end the war. They elected him president.

Neither side won the Korean War. Korea remained divided into North and South. Thousands of Americans, South Koreans, and UN allies were killed. Yet we had refused to let a small war grow into a big one.

Under their new president, Americans looked forward to the future with great hope.

Answer these to review the main ideas.

A.

1. What did the United States do when communist forces attacked

South Korea?_____

_____

_____

2. What happened when the United Nations drove the North Koreans back to the Chinese border? _____

_____

_____

3. How did President Truman and General MacArthur disagree about the way to fight the war? _____

_____

_____

4. How did the disagreement between Truman and MacArthur end?

_____

_____

5. What did General Eisenhower promise the American people he would do if they elected him president? _____

_____

_____

Circle the right answer to finish each sentence.

B.

1. The Korean War began in

   a. 1940   b. 1945   c. 1950

2. Most United Nations soldiers were

   a. Chinese   b. South Koreans and Americans   c. French and English

3. "There is no substitute for victory" was said by

   a. President Truman   b. General MacArthur   c. General Eisenhower

4. The Chinese Communists pushed the United Nations forces back to

   a. South Korea   b. North Korea   c. Japan

5. In World War II, General Eisenhower commanded American forces in

   a. Asia   b. North America   c. Europe

Circle True or False.

C.

T F 1. The communist forces helped North Korea, and the United Nations helped South Korea.

T F 2. The United Nations refused to take part in the Korean War.

T F 3. The North Korean army was poorly trained by the Soviet Union.

T F 4. General MacArthur said we had no right to bomb China.

T F 5. General Eisenhower was elected president of the United States.

Choose one of these words to fit each sentence below.

D.

truce   peninsula   polls

equipment   crisis

1. When Americans vote, they go to the _____.

2. A halt to the fighting in a war is called a _____.

3. Korea is on a _____, a piece of land almost surrounded by water.

4. That was a _____, a time when the war could be won or lost.

5. Soldiers need good _____ to carry out their duties.

Think about and discuss in class.

E.

Find out what is going on in Korea today. Is the United States still interested in helping South Korea maintain a democracy? _____

_____

_____

Why did President Truman remove General MacArthur from his command? _____

_____

Do you think this was the right thing for Truman to do? Explain. ____

_____

_____

_____

84

Was the Korean War worth fighting for the United States and its allies? _____

_____

_____

_____

Who *really* ran the war in Korea — the United States or the United Nations? _____

_____

_____

_____

_____

_____

_____

_____

Final Review Test

Here are fifteen vocabulary words you have learned while reading this book. Choose one word to fit each sentence below.

I.

satellite	candidate	prosperity
slums	conservation	assassinate
depression	enthusiastic	Reconstruction
trench	nominate	drought
credit	impeach	monopoly

1. When a country is rich, it enjoys _____.

2. If we buy something now and pay for it later, we are buying on _____.

3. John D. Rockefeller, the businessman, had a _____ on oil.

4. The moon is a _____ of the earth.

5. Presidents Lincoln and McKinley were both murdered, or _____d.

6. Soldiers in the First World War did a lot of fighting from _____es.

7. Rebuilding and restoring the South was a period of time called _____.

8. Americans went through very hard times during the _____ _____ of the 1930s.

9. A long period without any rain is a _____.

10. A person who runs for election to office is a _____.

11. Congress _____ed President Johnson for being guilty of high crimes.

12. A person like Teddy Roosevelt, who was energetic and eager to get things done, is _____.

13. Every four years, we choose or _____ candidates for president.

14. Houses in a city that are very poor and crowded are called _____.

15. Protecting our natural resources is called _____.

Circle the right answer to finish each sentence.   **II.**

1. The Fourteenth Amendment gave Blacks

   a. American   b. land grants   c. education benefits
      citizenship

2. Thomas A. Edison invented

   a. the cotton gin   b. the telephone   c. the electric
                                                      light bulb

3. When business and labor try to reach a settlement, they may take part in

   a. collective   b. striking   c. voting
      bargaining

4. Puerto Ricans are

   a. Spanish citizens   b. Cuban citizens   c. American citizens

5. The president who said "Speak softly and carry a big stick" was

   a. Abraham   b. Andrew Johnson   c. Theodore
      Lincoln   Roosevelt

6. The League of Nations was the idea of

   a. Winston   b. Woodrow   c. Joseph
      Churchill   Wilson   Stalin

7. In 1920, women won

   a. the right to work   b. the right to strike   c. the right to vote

8. Franklin Roosevelt became president of the United States in

   a. 1933   b. 1903   c. 1973

9. Adolf Hitler was

   a. prime minister   b. an American   c. dictator
      of England   general   of Germany

10. The first city hit by an atomic bomb was

   a. London,   b. Paris, France   c. Hiroshima, Japan
      England

11. Winston Churchill of England said that Europe was divided by

   a. the Rhine River   b. the Axis Powers   c. an iron curtain

12. The first country to join the United Nations was

   a. England   b. the United States   c. the Soviet Union

13. The Korean War began in

   a. 1950   b. 1939   c. 1914

14. Most United Nations soldiers in the Korean War were

   a. Chinese   b. French and   c. Americans and
                           English   South Koreans

Circle True or False.

III.

T F 1. Carpetbaggers were often greedy Northerners who went south
          to make money after the Civil War.

T F 2. The United Nations stopped the iron curtain in Europe.

T F 3. Texas cowboys drove their cattle north to railroad towns
          and ranches on the Great Plains.

T F 4. General George Custer defeated Tatanka Yotanka and other
          Native Americans at the Battle of the Little Bighorn in 1876.

T F 5. Except for Native Americans, every American is either an
          immigrant or comes from a family who were once
          immigrants.

T F 6. President Franklin Roosevelt did not believe in spending
          government money to end the Great Depression.

T F 7. In World War II, the Japanese bombed Pearl Harbor,
          Hawaii. This brought the United States into the war.

T F 8. The United States fought alone against the communist forces
          in Korea.

Match the words in the first column with the correct definition in the second column. Draw a line between each word or name and its meaning.

IV.

Reconstruction	Franklin Roosevelt's program to end the Great Depression
the Rough Riders	World peace-keeping force
Gertrude Ederle	Struggle for power between communist and democratic countries
the New Deal	Commanded by Teddy Roosevelt in Spanish-American War
the Cold War	Went to California during Great Depression
Dwight Eisenhower	Period after the Civil War when the North rebuilt the South
United Nations	Invented the telephone in 1876
Marshall Plan	Army commander who became President of the United States
Oklahoma "Okies"	Rebuilt Western Europe after Second World War
Alexander Graham Bell	Swam the English Channel in 1926

In your own words, write about one of the American presidents in this book. What kind of a person was he? What were some of the things he did? Use this book to help you.

V.